Do Not Enter Alarmed Area

Nigel Hutchinson

Cinnamon Press
:: small miracles from distinctive voices ::

Published by Cinnamon Press
www.cinnamonpress.com

ISBN 978-1-78864-110-4

British Library Cataloguing in Publication Data. A CIP record for this book can be obtained from the British Library.

Designed and typeset in Bodoni by Cinnamon Press. Cover design by Adam Craig © Adam Craig.

Cinnamon Press is represented by Inpress

Acknowledgements

Thanks to Stratford upon Avon Stanza group for comments on the stirrings of this book, Christine, Liz and Luke again, Aysar Ghassan for walking and talking the trail, Liz Jolly for Barber visits, Fiona Venables and Sarah Shalgosky at the Mead Gallery, University of Warwick, Mike Tooby and the 'Journeys With The Waste Land' Research Group and apologies to B for lack of rhyme (again).

'Feed Me Now' first appeared in *Acumen*. 'Cézanne the Optician', 'A Warning from the Art Police' first appeared in *Equinox*. 'Hitch-Hiking' first appeared on the *Writers' Café* website. An earlier version of 'Beyond the Haywain' appears in *From Hallows to Harvest*, Cinnamon Press. An earlier version of 'Caterpillar & Diver' appeared in *The North*. An earlier version of 'A Warning from the Art Police' appeared in *Cake*. An earlier version of 'Postcard: New Mexico with Georgia O'Keeffe' first appeared in *New Contexts:1*. 'An Attempt to Define the Smell of Wood Sap', 'Interpreting the Past', 'Obelisks I Imagine Are Meant to Pierce the Sky', 'Let's Not Be Stupid', 'Jake Makes A Dinosaur Model', 'Lucy Tomlin's Concrete Country Makes Me Wonder', 'Shadows and Light', 'Regret Not an Original Sin', 'Some Equations for Making A Hare', 'It's A Question of', 'On This Day'—written for the sculpture trail at the University of Warwick/Mead Gallery website. 'Bronze Cannot Fly', 'It's on the Tip of Your Tongue', 'Everyone's Daughter', 'All Hands on Deck', 'Is That James Joyce...', 'One of Those Nights'—written for the exhibition 'Journeys with The Waste Land', Herbert Art Gallery, Coventry.

Contents

For Keir, may he always have gumption

Do Not Enter Alarmed Area

Do Not Enter Alarmed Area

after a sign at the Barber Institute of Fine Arts, Birmingham University

In the event of becoming alarmed management
suggest that patrons refrain from running
and avoid panic by making their way
to a painting of their choice.

We would recommend contemplating
the Sea Arch At Etretat, perhaps
the Church At Varennes, or the golden glow
of a Pastoral Landscape.

Those recently bruised in love
are advised to avoid
Lovers In A Landscape
and The Flavour Of Tears.

Visitors disturbed by violence
should not seek out
The Beheading Of John The Baptist
or Judith With The Head Of Holofernes.

The agitated should imagine themselves
on the beach with Bather's At Tahiti
or boarding The Harvest Wagon tired
but satisfied as the day's work ends.

In the event of entering an *Alarmed Area*
remain calm, if fatalistic remember
Portrait Of A Man Holding A Skull,
if not, the promise of Jockeys Before A Race.

Not Quite Daydreaming

after A Woman Seated In a Garden (*La Songeuse*), *Toulouse Lautrec*

In summer there are lilacs
they catch the early light before
sun has made them fragrant.

This is the time cat walks
along the wall, licks the air,
stretches, settles.

Now these streets are reborn,
last night swept and washed away,
the business of today delivered—
bread, newspapers, wine and hope

—not quite hope, maybe a sense that
there was a victory over yesterday—
or at least a truce.

Today I am still my own witness,
this work will pass, only a coat
I can slip off, discard.

Cat will walk these paths,
brush my leg just enough
to be complicit.

Later he will arrive to draw
my profile, tell me again
my pale skin and marmalade hair
glow in this violet shadow

—he's a liar like me
using every crutch he can.

In summer there are lilacs
they catch the light as it fades
cat returns to its fireside
stretches, settles.

Barbara Hepworth's Eye

after Four Figures, *Barbara Hepworth*

These four figures conjured into being
with confidence of line, economy of pencil
a wrist's flex and flow—

as if a latent film, flicker-book surprise
as if *you* can do some of this work
as if the day is starting again and again...

as if they're auditioning to be classical statues
as if they're remembering 50's film stars
as if these women cannot be erased

Those feet at once rooted
and about to move weightlessly—
there's a grace here

how to hold yourself
how to exit a scene
turn an ankle, turn away

Though only pencilled in
they're practised as those diagrams
of feet learning dance steps

or are these women at ancient wells
confident as the Bible, certain as myth
stepped from Pre-Raphaelite paintings

carrying the heft of history
witnesses to stoicism, certainty, endurance
somewhere at the back of Hepworth's eye.

Christian Kobke Painting Frederick Soding

It occurs to me that this is
some kind of incest—
I'm painting him painting in
his mind's eye.

Seated in that chair
he's facing me, though look at his legs—
he'd rather be off, leaving
a Frederik-shaped absence -

me a fellow conspirator
compliant illusionist confined
to airless, polished rooms
those niceties of conversation

him in long coat and rain-rattled hat
(brush welded to his flexible hand)
soaked in the landscape
his eyes are drinking.

An Attempt to Define the Smell of Wood Sap

after the willow sculpture Don't Let Go, *Laura Ellen Bacon, Warwick University* *campus*

It's hard to grasp
something on the edge
between sweet and savoury

presence and almost absence
a lure perhaps, an enticement...
breathing in never quite enough

Maybe this scent some
childhood memory when
an adult life was a mystery

cycle rides on slow afternoons
warm air that slips past your face
timelessness kissing your body

palpable fragrance of sunlight
through dappled leaves
promise of sleep's satisfactions

Perhaps nothing so clearly defined
just a sense that this fragility
hangs in the balance, more easily
ignored than savoured.

The Same Soil

for the man up a tree in the background of Two Peasants Binding Faggots, *Pieter Brueghel the Younger*

He's always been the quiet one
the boy who gazed beneath the surface
of pond and stream, easily transfixed
by mirrored clouds drifting
across the skin of another world

now a peasant up a ladder cutting
kindling, high enough to look
beyond the wood's dark interior
much further than today—

       to the west seeing a red-haired man
       intense as rain, painting the earthiness
       of boots and potatoes, watching him
       burst into colour, burst into flame

       to the north an artist drawing trees
       until he finds the rhythm of them,
       a surgeon pruning back to a truth
       of horizontals, verticals, primary colours…

Cutting firewood *his* day's evidence
hands and body set to the task
some other part of him
wondering what *he* might have been
grown from this same soil

Postcard:
Karouin, Morocco

Here with Paul Klee taking his famous
line for a walk, like tourists setting off
into the unknown, without a definite plan.
We're here by design, patterns of trees
and houses stacked on hillsides make much
more sense now he's reduced them to the
obvious—can't see this place without seeing
his spidery line, watercolour world.
Reminded that lines we walk with dogs,
bicycles, work, follow habits lodged in our
automatic footsteps—after all we've all drawn
distinctions and conclusions with confidence
if not pen, pencil or colour. Hope this finds
you in the pink X

Postcard:
Giverny, lessons in colour theory

for Theo, the boy with complementary socks

a yellow day
a boy wearing
one red
one green sock
walks between irises
maybe Monet smiling
exclaiming that air
is violet

an officious man
in French blue trousers
shouts at picnickers
through a megaphone
while orange nasturtiums
complement him
and shout back
quietly

The Cling of Clay

after Guests At A Wedding, *Pieter Breughel the Elder*

Bagpiper—the necessary man—librarian of tunes
dancing master, swirls the dancers' bulky bodies
wildness in the wail of drones—

he leads them on
into mischief and out of themselves
beyond the cling of clay

Against the wall a rounded man
black hat framing his tilting head
stands out on the edge

sees shadows, looks to the piper
who pulls invisible strings.
They've swung and swayed

spun themselves to the height of spirits
a congregation of limbs
in the flow of feet over too solid earth

as lost as each other in this dance of drink
the rules of misrule—this is today
tomorrow a flatter-footed dance.

Lowry's Inferno

Mills recede into yellowed air
these grainy-walled canyons overshadow
harsh sparks of clogs clocking on, clocking off

Wind cuts in from the Pennines
grubby stubble between flagstones
cemetery flowers struggling for breath

Collar turned, trilby-hatted rentman collects
memorises this labyrinth of creeping terraces
back alleys, shops full of gossip

pubs looking for an argument
A three-coloured country, ochre, brick, slate
relieved by specks of scarlet

Salford's Dante treads sulphurous streets
sketching those who mustn't complain
mustn't grumble

Postcard:
Japanese Garden—raining

—the view reminds me of that print,
two travellers crossing a bridge
with hopeful umbrellas,
another under a wide-brimmed hat.
Waterman's boat a lone horizontal—
all of them as fleeting as rainstorms.
Showers vertical as gravity, then just
that dance of rain on water.
Now onomatopoeic lake swallowing
a frog.

P.S a heron just rose clean into the evening sky
like an omen.

Postcard:
Paris, Tuesday

Someone has sprayed the arms of
shop dummies gold, hung them
in this café window—
some latterday Surrealist?—
arms that once wore elegant dresses
naked in the shady air.
At tables beneath these golden limbs
men drinking dreams,
young women reading this year's news,
what to wear, who to be.

Beyond the Haywain

On placemats and tea towels it's a rustic idyl
sunlit cornfields, carthorse, a rippling river
sky high and rolling
—a national flag for bucolic England

but if you count the people
this cornfield is a factory
dozens of white smocks labouring
relentless harvesters of daily bread

Out of sight it's not so green
or pleasant, cuts in wages, rising prices
machinery discarding men
riots, rick burnings, desperation

Philip De Loutherbourg in Coalbrookdale

after Coalbrookdale at Night, *Philip de Loutherbourg*

These first furnaces smelted a self-made man
from ore, coke, pitiless heat and labourers' sweat—
men thrown into shadows against a billowing night sky
Abraham Derby lighting the blue touchpaper of a new world

Wonder if De Loutherbourg felt himself prophetic
or if shades of the inferno ever crossed his theatrical mind
such energy here, such undermining of the past
a future promised, fortune chanced

Nearby the Brays and Baughs whose ashy genes I carry
hewing the fuel to stoke these fires, excavating a living
driven by that other primal force
the silent voice of generations waiting to be born.

Wild Beasts & Symbolists

after Portrait of Bartolomeo Savona, *André Derain* & Portrait of Arthur Huc,
Maurice Denis

Savona sits for an hour as Derain the Fauve
constructs his portrait from short brushstrokes
tubes of pure pigment, decisive as a wild beast.
Sharp-suit, cool grey and white striped tie emerge
blue-black hair frames the firm-jawed face—
he is built, made present through paint

Nearby, Arthur Huc, hand draped over
the edge of his chair, unconscious cigarette
red-tipped against black, properly relaxes
with hair still neat, glasses studious
inside Maurice Denis' composition
content to be colours in a certain order

At first the conversation wears formal collars
tidy ties, Bartolomeo explaining the intoxication
of colour 'like sticks of dynamite'
Arthur—they're on first name terms now—
the search for something more, subtle
and unseen under the surface.

Postcard:
Vitebsk, dusk

Marc and Bella still floating over houses.
Reminded me of that dancer—the one
who spun until he was as solid as a blur.
No one breathed. For a moment anything
seemed possible. We'd forgotten how
earthbound our bodies could be
filled with something much heavier than
lead, stone or history.

PS—you know who I mean, don't you?

Standing on the Beach

after The Beach At Trouville, *Eugene Boudin*
i.m Aylan Kurdi

I am salt on lips, ozone in nostrils
the rolling of seas, grains on a beach

storm and lapping wave
windblown, scoured, bleached

foreigner, flotsam, migrant
calcium and carbon

skeleton, shell and shroud
mineral and animate

all the oceans of the world
I am memory in your spiralled ear

on the edge between
you and time

on the edge between
you and nothing that matters

on the edge between
you and a boy on a beach

The Sound of the Sea

after Vanitas, *Harmen Steenwyck*

Steenwyck taps you on your shoulder
you turn
see the painting he's pointing at

a still life on a table, books, pocket watch
brass lamp, musical instruments
sword, skull, coiled shell

The skull is turned towards you
that laughing gape and hollow eyes—
you know about mortality, wonder about the rest

The books have no titles—
knowledge as fragile as memory
Music no longer even an echo

Power of the wealthy sword—temporary
timepiece tells of time elapsed
lamp's smoke coils upwards—evaporates...

everything points to that conch
separate at the table edge, you lift it
put it to you ear, listen...

No Man's Land

after Totes Meer, *Paul Nash*

Shipwrecked sea stitched
to an ochre beach
sky a shepherd's delight
moon sharp

as a gunsight
waves breaking steely cold
pebbles suck and pull
quiet as camouflage

Morning paused
except a preying owl
patrolling the struggle
between shoreline and sea

Now a different tide hauls
onto John Donne's continent
fugitives from deadly dances
of faith and power

Interpreting the Past

after Forest Planet, *Atsuo Okamoto, University of Warwick campus*

To be clear, this is not Pompeii
These are not ash-cloud mummies
vaporised lives, although there is
something of that unexpected moment

Under the tree canopy volcanic bombs
cooled to granite density, three boulder-like forms
transported from another age
a different place, though

they may be shape-shifters, egg cases after
what was life has burst into being, worm casts
or burrowings on some ancient beach
perhaps unseen seed pods, redundant relics

Whatever their history they're both raw
and polished, bursting or exploded
threats like landmines or husks like
conker shells in autumn

Now Frost Falls on Stilled Snow, Sky A Bitter Grey

after Hunters In The Snow, *Pieter Breughel the Elder, for B*

Villagers skate the river's polished highway
on ponds they fish through ice cold as a grudge
they will land eels and silver-sided fish
skin and fillet the season's bare bones

Over the hill men with good intentions
are pressing through drifts, leaning into winter
hunger they carry like the weight of an animal

they'll pass the transformation of a pig—
not quite a resurrection—but the trading
of one heartbeat for another

With butchery's efficient habit saws and blades
are cleaving, nothing will be lost
from blood to bone a woman is carving
carving a life; raising the knife, cutting to the heart

skinning and stripping, flex and turn of her wrists
heft of her arms learned from her mother
her mother's mother and back through generations

Easy skill her way with the world, it is only material
to be conquered, turned to use
Accusing eyes of the pig no match for the eyes
of a hungry stomach

By day's end, when cold will have reached her marrow
there will be strings of sausage, blood pudding
sides of meat smoking, bones for skates, sinew for thread
she will take off her bloody, sacrificial apron, survivor's armour

Postcard:
Ah, Siena

There is much that is Baroque here—
marble columns, gold leaf pulpits as if
decoration were next to godliness.
Left the last church feeling
I'd eaten too much rich food. Later
the sky framed inside a window
boiling with golden clouds rolling
into the pink of shells, lead of thunder.
Then these nimbus towers the stage
for a theatre of lightning,
better than Rococo fireworks!

Postcard:
Weekend, Assisi?

Saw this and thought of you.
There are dog whisperers here.
And rumours. Dog arrived
with something in its paw.
A man talked to it gently,
removed a thorn. Later
one of them remembered
St Jerome—or was it Francis?
The dog continues to visit.
Expects biscuits.

The Purpose of Holidays

after Killary Bay Connemara, *Paul Henry*

The plan was to navigate the map's edge
until the road ran out, reach furthest
points south—west—north

perfect strands negotiated daily
between sand and sea
under the quiet drama of clouds rolling

travel mute past the forgotten language
of standing stones, sky-roofed houses
hillsides ribbed with broken walls

to watch sun melt sea to bronze
be far enough away
to look back

Obelisks I Imagine Are Meant to Pierce the Sky

after the sculpture Needle Of Knowledge, *Stefan Knapp, University of Warwick campus*

point the way to somewhere
or maybe from then to *now*
They're statements of intent
instructions to get up and away
freed from gravity, the weight of *here*
those ideas about perfectibility
things that seem to matter
You and I shrinking—
too small to figure out the presence of people

At this height not even dots on a landscape
as if the telescope's reversed
suddenly everything so far away and yet
so sharp, so bright

In these enamelled aerial memories of earth
topography of hill, river, woodland mapped
in paintbox fresh colours
wiped of waste, spoil, disappointment
Trail of abandonment and abuse scrubbed
clean, brightened by what seems like delight
as if every city, town and village is yearning for
endlessly changing dances with only wind and water
arced by rainbows, rinsed with sky's simplicity

Negotiations

after Cornwall, *Ben Nicholson*

Sometimes it's hard to tell where land
ends, water ceases, sea and sky separate
this peninsula a leg stepping out
braving grey swell and swirl, dipping its toe
wondering how the day will swim

earlier a couple on this beach
arm in arm and more, anxious
to know the flow of each other, what is
granite, what as constant as a westerly

above, a farmhouse shouldered against the hill
semaphore washing telling stories
in shirts, socks and sheets
a family's waxing and waning

seagulls and rooks stitching clouds to rolling air
mobbing the distant noise of a red tractor
ploughing straight lines on the turn of the earth

true and clear furrows mapping contours
claiming possession of heath and thicket
striking a temporary deal with wilderness

Bronze Cannot Fly

after Bird, *Elizabeth Frink*

This twisted wreck tarred, oil-slicked
to some unknown runway
desperate to rise and glide
it staggers

flesh, meat such fragile stuff
stripped away, *carne*, carnage

drags itself forward, a death-throw bomber
undercarriage legs crippled
fluid flight now shattered sheets of metal
a different skin, the end of feathered flight

plumage
            plunge
                        plummet

Hare Arrests Time

for Roz Goddard
after the sculpture Acrobats, *Barry Flanagan*

That critical moment—
you two Hares, one balancing the other
just after *then* but before... *now*

held for a breath these magicians of time
at the point where we all might applaud
try to believe our eyes, hold on...

someone runs her hand up Hare's bronze back
cups his tail, strokes his thigh, ignore this familiarity
do not be distracted, hold on Hare.

Someone tries to climb Hare's back, hold his ears
like reins, tame him between wilful legs
—ignore them Hare.

Buck on his toes, doe walking clouds
Hare's eye to Hare's eye in anticipation
a supernatural telepathy, acute to every sound.

Hold on Hare—you touch the ground lightly
effortlessly leap, turn, change direction
sometimes just for the hell of it...

dance your stories, perform your virile magic
it's not you that's mad—you're immortal
you're moon's little god, talisman

Ploughs and combines comb your earth
economies of scale, hard-nosed profit margins
praise an ever-rising graph, a paltry satisfaction

Do not be distracted, hold on Hare, hold on
you should be running, not for your life
but the sheer delight of it

Expect you to bow gracefully, then
race off across fields
Something inside us, leaping

Daphne and Apollo

after Daphne Pursued by Apollo & The Metamorphosis of Daphne, *The Paris Master c1450*

We cannot see the crow police
noting the ways of women
methods of men
what schemes, what wiles

her heading for shelter
him blundering on intent
on the chase
bramble and thorn scratching
calf, hand and arm
crashing through thickets
pursuing the game
his appetite.

Crow watches with camera eyes
raises the alarm—

but this turning into a tree—
why her, not him?

Let's Not Be Stupid

after Let's Not Be Stupid, *Richard Deacon*

sun sparkles surfaces into galaxies
unimaginable distances deep in a steel sky—
this holds momentarily

then the reality of bolts and engineering
plus the memory of a feint smell—
oil, ghosts of factories

let's not be stupid—it's all steel of course
but easy to see this drawing-in-air
could be deforming softly, reforming

performing dramas large and small
not hard as tempered metal
but soft as a graphite pencil

let's not fool ourselves, skies will change
but monochrome is always black and white—
something about the choices we're offered

Meanwhile Deacon's roiling curves frame
a traffic island declaring a cacophony
of poppies, cornflowers, a protest march

against serious stuff you can bark shins on
gash and bruise yourself—can red really be
that red, blue be so calm, grass so vivid?

discords, complementaries putting up a fight
against such substantial materiality, we'd be
stupid, foolish to dismiss play and interplay

Cézanne the Optician

'Monet is only an eye but, my god, what an eye', Paul Cézanne

Time held between breaths
by the shutter of his eye
in the economy of his darting wrist

him wishing that the world was new
every morning, wanting to discover again
that air was violet, strokes of colour are all
we see, shimmering.

We can smell the French air
sunlight on gardens, know that
water, sky, land are only the colour of light
besieging our eyes—
flame-red haystacks cast sage-green shadow
cool blue frost haunts burnt-orange trees
pale lemon light licks violet snow

that the presence of paint
is not an imitation of the world
but how it is when stripped of familiarity
alive like the sharpness of winter in nostrils
intimacy of sun on skin

Its on the Tip of Your Tongue

after Fairground, *Barbara Jones*

but memory falters
those threads that ran
through scenes so clearly
have retreated—
only a particular calm
mute as a swansong

                  hesitates

across scoured landscapes
between houses and shadow trees
hovers over frozen seas
fairgrounds on Sunday morning
horses caught mid-leap
as if making choices

Postcard:
Oslo with E.M.

An awesome sunset!
like pennants before a battle
fjord on fire—glorious—
heard his scream before
we saw him, a silhouette
blocking our path—
didn't sound like anger
or frustration, more the end
of a tether, him an animal
out of options, like he was
drowning on dry land
someone waved—
brought back memories.
Still didn't know what to do.

Postcard:
Kochel with Kandinsky, Monday

The painting overleaf is accurate
to the extent that there's a graveyard
and there has been snow—
not a dusting, but the kind
that brightens your eyes,
makes your nostrils burn,
air fill with that special sound
as large balls of snow are rolled,
transformed into knowing men
with coal-dark eyes.
You should have seen them

P.S thanks for the thermal socks

What Are the Chances?

after portraits by Percy Wyndham Lewis, words by Bob Dylan & Ezra Pound

Portraits of Pound and Eliot hang
side by side—a revelation—
muscular forms sharp as an editor's knife

I quote the line about them fighting
in the captain's tower, the woman
next to me completes the couplet

we turn, exclaim
'Dylan'
together recite the next line—

we've travelled thousands
of miles to be here now
both of us transformed

into the teenagers we were—
evening rooms, same records
high on words

she in some city out west
me dreaming desolation and desire
days and nights not full enough

no thought that life might slip by
like Ezra Pound's mouse
grass remain unshaken

Feed Me Now

after Five Welsh Chapels, *John Piper*

Everything here is clear
foundations set in solid certainties
no Gothic exuberance, staining glass
or Baroque indulgence; non-conformity
mapped with Old Testament precision—
Bethel, Bethesda, Salem, Zion

Belief is the colour of slate
blacker than Dylan's Bible, even
on a cloudless night
miners' lamps, quarriers' ropes hanging
on the bread of heaven, harmonies sure
as the rock they've hewn and hauled

Now chapels lead less certain lives
Evermore sold to the highest bidder
low rent for carpets, curios
conversion opportunities
Salvation postponed, Palestine
partitioned

Everyone's Daughter

after History Snap 1 *(1984), Terry Atkinson , and* 'The Terror Of War', photo of Kim Phuc 1972, *Nick Ut*

Cannot help but see the echo of *that* photograph
young girl running towards us burning with napalm
she hovers in our history—this again
connecting, connecting, maybe it's the same child

who watched snipers and burning tyres
from a broken window
was carried from Syrian rubble
caught the glint of light on a machete

ran from a cloud she'd never seen before
saw lines of soldiers machine-marching
towards trenches and annihilation
ran through snow from Napoleon's army

migrated, a refugee with Mother Courage
across the wastelands of the world
this again and againandagain

The Timing of Vengeance

after Judith and Holofernes, *Artemisia Gentileschi*

At five to the hour her maid's arms
force down his body onto the bed
point to the halved hour

clock ticks

His right arm pushes upwards
to midnight, to her face, impassive
at this critical hour, the tipping point

clock ticks

at ten past her outstretched arms
grip the pivot of this night's work
his head

clock ticks

Judith slices the sword she holds
anticlockwise
halts time, severs his neck

clock ticks

his face, his eyes turned
beyond the hand's swing
straining for the rising hour

clock ticks
blood flows like hourglass sand
his time ticks

tick
tic
ti
t

Jake Makes A Dinosaur Model

after The Good and The Bad, *Jake & Dinos Chapman, University of Warwick campus, October 2019. (Originally titled 'The Meek Shall Inherit The Earth, But Not The Mineral Rights')*

it looks like a tyrannosaurus rex
Dinos assembles a plywood stegosaurus
—both surprised how huge they turn out
when they're made in steel—
too big for bedroom or kitchen table

but not as shocked as the great crested newts
watching from the pond's edge, discussing how
events have unfolded, tricks evolution plays—
who'd have thought they'd survive to give
this patch of earth a cold-blooded stare

Down the slope bright yellow diggers
performing animatronic dances
like a makeshift tribute act
skeins of geese perform textbook landings
—pterodactyl ghosts with ancient voices

crow can only call and caw
perch on a dinosaur spine like a harbinger
our newts slip back into undergrowth
consider what exactly the meek will inherit
and what the future holds for mineral rights

Half A Millennium Ago Albrecht Dürer Paints A Hare

His eyes, acute as any buck's or jill's
study the roll and curve of its muscular landscape
downland pregnant with the moment

watch the breathing universe of its body
flex and latent kick of those folded haunches
taut as survival, taunt of hound and hunter

Hare's eyes miss nothing
see threat in the air like a crackle of lightning
ears radar-scan soundwaves

those ways and wiles of men
snares and spells, secret names
and incantations

Dürer matching every bristle
with sympathetic brushstrokes—
conjuring in an age of familiars.

Look at how he paints himself—
same attention to texture of hair
and his fur-collared coat

him a shape-shifting hare, perhaps
—Albrecht, all bright-eyed
determined to miss nothing

Concerning the Gravity of A Sculpted Brass Head

after Eastre (Hymn To The Sun), *J.D Fergusson*

Lines of her face bold
planes delineated, sharp as Spring
I can see me in her, surprisingly bright
stretched in her neck
like a fairground

I'm washed out denim
bronzed face and hands
forehead burnished
shadows something between
suntan and darker memories

Reflection on the plinth
like a veined moth's wing
so much less certain
than the gravity of her head
temporal as an easter egg

Casting Yourself in Bronze

after Head Of Sir Osbert Sitwell, *bronze and its plaster maquette, Frank Dobson*

Curves of his face taut and glowing
angles tensile, clean-edged
planes decisive, refined

he's streamlined and polished
smooth as an operator
the world's troubles should flow

past without turbulence
that nose a prow cutting ill winds
hair sleek as sealskin

it's a public head worn
for bust and portrait
he will not be the man

who lost himself
his patrician eyes seem
not to see the plaster maquette

that prefigured this shining self
its scuffs and scars
patching and stains

the blood that is a fragile tree
we carry within us

Lines 12 & 13: The Man Who Lost Himself, *the title of Sitwell's second novel*
Lines 19 & 20: after a remark by Sitwell

Caterpillar & Diver

after Vase of Flowers, *Jan de Heem*

Spot the caterpillar turning leaves to lace
then a pupa discreetly hidden
biding its time

a butterfly completes this trinity
flutters upwards
liberated from this material world

Remember that falling figure
plunging into death like someone diving
into life, unskinned

naked in thickening air
high above the debris of certainty
an acrobat tumbling free

expect him to open wings
glide into the morning
a man in his own hands, mythic butterfly

Points of View

after The Wrath Of Ahaseuras, *Jan Steen*

Dog wears a small bell, whoever tied its red ribbon
is charmed by this, dog's faithful following jingling
quieter than the dramas of ostentatious men

Dog keeps its distance, wiser than Parrot
who merely repeats the rage of powerful leaders
their tweetings, flammable outbursts, self obsession

acute-eared Dog hears a goblet shatter
spoon clatter, considers its unnoticed advantage
as falling salver and peacock amplify this drama

though Dog does not care for chef's skills, or hours
of preparation—a meal is a meal—those on the
margins must take what they can

Dog smells roasted flesh, not Jan Steen's unsubtle
Symbolism—those all-seeing peacock-tail-eyes
of someone's god -

Dog's only focus the coming powerplay
between roasted flesh
and canine teeth

Still, Life

after Still Life With Musical Instruments, *Evaristo Baschenis*

This is the point at which
the player has stopped playing

soundbox and body cease
reverberating

last vibration of strings drifts
beyond hearing

notes from the mouth of shawm
and singer decay

tellingly placed peach
silently blooms, that moment

between teeth breaking
its skin and burst of juice

All Hands on Deck

after Trystan and Esyllt, *David Jones*

Even if you don't know the opera, or Celtic myth
Trystan and Essyllt and their oh-so-close alter egos
Tristan and Isolde are still all at sea

the captain wondering how many marriages
weather storms, how many go through rocky patches
hit the rocks, run aground, ignore siren voices

Overwhelmed by ego and hormones
the tide of things sweeping them out of their depth
leaving them adrift without oars or sail

Even if arias are explanations or therapy
the chorus is drowned out by crashing waves
and the simple impetus of dramas set in train

Who can stand on the shore and light signal fires
shout loud enough to turn back
tides of unfolding events—

is that the thing about tragedy?
needing to prepare ourselves
for moments when the mast breaks

we're left rudderless and uncertain
buying ourselves time before decisions hit us
in our faces like rakes we might accidentally step on?

The Label Says the Flute

after Two Peasants Binding Faggots, *Pieter Breughel*

is a symbol - maybe phallic?
Look, there's a scrotal fold
in his green trousers
and that vulval tear near his knee
he must be—lechery!

The other man's appetite
has strained his shirt
and passionate red trousers
Gluttony written all around his waistline

Then there's their mate thieving branches
from a tree that could be a cross, or gibbet...

they're gathering wood against winter
unaware of the moral symbolism of their lives
the lessons that can be taught beyond
the practical skills of tying knots
and getting by

Postcard:
Sunday in the park with Léger

He'd have us live in a halted world
balance happening suddenly.
Sometimes things fall into place.
People unpainting everything
they've chosen to forget,
the moment when the 'snow'
you've shaken in one of those domes
settles back as if you were just
a passing flurry.

Postcard:
Figueras, failing to avoid Dali

In this landscape of lamps and bushes
he has perfected the art of balancing
them on his head. There are no strings.
His shoulders resemble
a snow capped peak, skiers are racing
down his arms—but this is not his fate
he is digging holes he carefully fills
with finest sand, remembering how
sunlight dazzled him on the beach
when sand slipped down the hourglass
like a woman's waist.

P.S.—remember the ice cream?

A Warning from the Art Police

Unnerving to see them
two sisters or identical friends
looking like they'd been drawn by Tenniel

emerged from Alice In Wonderland
wandered through a Paula Rego painting
and out onto the street—
off with his head ringing in their ears.

Who else has slipped quietly
out of the frame, is at large amongst us
without warning?

How long before gallery walls are empty
no longer display portraits and narratives
streets swelling with faces we recognise
but can't quite place...

Venus in the sunbed lounge
Gauguin in the travel agent
Toulouse-Lautrec at the theatre
Mona Lisa in Tesco.

Is That James Joyce...

after If Not, Not, *R.B Kitaj, and* The Shore, *Paul Nash*

in the arms of a Tahitian woman out of Gauguin
and who's the bearded figure in bed, like some ancient of days
measuring or sheering a fleece, stone head at his feet with
a look of confusion on its face, some toppled statue
fallen like the red-coated soldiers, prone or dead
and that forlorn figure despondent beneath a blasted tree?

  they're all alone, lost in thought or, simply lost...

why the sole sheep sheltering beneath
a stunted trunk, no flock to follow
one palm—some oasis in this post-apocalypse
other trees like chimneys, leaves of smoke,
Birkenau above a turquoise pool
beside a chrome yellow sulphurous hill and leaching sky?

  I'm all alone now, lost in thought or...

crawling soldier dreams of reaching the top of the brow
to gaze over an unexpected beach, the coast of somewhere,
sea from elsewhere shackled to the moon's imperative,
colour is bleaching sand slipping to the seabed,
sand that washes beneath waves all the way to France,
the continental edge

  I'm all alone...

time slides not with clocks but tides and ebb,
time and space measured by breakwaters
attempting to defy the flux of hours,
concrete defences, sea walls, hunkered down
against a shining ocean,
sky grey as our grasp of the future, our clouded vision

  is this what brought us here...

concreting the island's edges to keep them out?
Low cloud hangs and the fear
that out of it will come that droning again,
ghosts of birds heavier than air blundering overhead,
speaking tongues we do not understand

      soldiers have gone...

Imagine a bucket-&-spaded child,
first onto the arc of the bay
construction and disaster in its eyes—

beach is deserted
no faith anymore
in sand castles

Toothache and Other Incidents

after Portrait of Bartolomeo Savona, *André Derain*, Mère Poussepin, *Gwen John*, The Evening Meal, *Pierre Bonnard*, Paolo and Francesca, *Ingres*, The Beheading of John the Baptist, *Puvis de Chavannes*, St Jerome in the Wilderness, *Bellini*, St John the Baptist Leaving for the Desert, *Neri di Bicci*

Bartolomeo Savona talking with André Derain about toothache
him complaining in expletive-laden French,
we decide to find a dentist without delay
if only to calm his temper, but are met on the doorstep
by Gwen John arm in arm with Mère Poussepin,
recently relieved of a tooth and several hundred francs

André's nerve fails him,
dabbing the last of the clove oil on his gums
we turn on our down at heels, tumble into Old Bonnard
furtively sketching a woman and her daughters
through an open window
he acting like an innocent, us suspicious, unconvinced
Derain reminds us of the Ingres painting around the corner
Gianciotto appearing out of the shadows, drawing his sword to end
wife Francesca's dalliance with his brother Paolo

I have a flashback—a sword swinging
towards the neck of John The Baptist
—surprised to see him looking like Russell the librarian—
until finally he is cast into the desert with only a camel skin,
a raging toothache
and a feeling that there have been better days than this,
days with lions
without thorns.

Doorstep Blues

after Cliff Dwellers, *George Bellows*

Thanks for the postcard, guess you're in New York
didn't say before you left and, yes
I remember those days—
who was that girl always doing handstands?

I tried over and over—
and those cartwheels she turned—
something about the way she could turn life upside
down and didn't seem to care

best I could do was lie on my back
imagine walking on the ceiling,
door frames like a boat's, never solved
problems of lampshades, curtains, gravity

D'you know what happened to the man who played clarinet
and that woman with the violin—they were going
somewhere, always looking up the street
said one day they'd be out of here

Saw her once, bag over her shoulder
ticket still in her eyes...

Trudge

after Snowy Landscape at Chatou, *Andre Derain*

Iced with snow for days now, houses
settle under cushions fluffed for winter

distance washed a starving evening blue
sun bleeds lower and quickly lower

stark trees line the road
briefly blazing scarlet

a deadened clock strikes
measures the crumping of his boots

him a silhouette
imagining fire

Fire at Its Heart

after Rain, Steam and Speed—The Great Western Railway, *JMW Turner*

Engulfed by steam, heart beating fast
hare crosses the tracks, panics
as the future arrives on iron rails

ore and coal hewn from the earth
fuel this speed of change
this elemental alchemy

engine's wheeze and puff
sloughing off driving rain
carving scars, blazing trails

fire at its heart our train travels on
cleaving the air, shrinking distance
sparking revolutions

Seeing Is Not Necessarily...

after American Gothic, *Grant Wood*

Him and her stiffly posed
upright as pitchforks
lean as salt, severe and simple

you'd guess stern-faced Biblical names
Ruth and Luke, Mary and Moses
maybe puritanical Patience and Luther

they stand outside their farm
mouths ruled straight with discipline
she deferring to him, her eyes

like milk, cold and opaque
him a steely-framed hawk
buttoned like a pastor

workers in the holy orders
of toil, tillage, husbandry
dusting, baking, making do

both thin as a presbyterian bed
scrubbed sharp and shining
something next to godliness, though

they're only propagandist tools, deceivers
make believers, postman and his sister
acting out an American myth

Lucy Tomlins' Concrete Country Makes Me Wonder...

after Concrete Country In Red, *Lucy Tomlins*

The invitation is to climb, though
this ancient field edge long since
grubbed up, path that cut across
no longer in need of a stile

this steel replica as if to compensate
men with scythe or spade
who crossed here to perform
agriculture's seasonal rituals

maybe trysting evening lovers
slipping from farm to thicket
some urgency in their climbing
tang of transgression in their hearts

wear of boot on wood, polish of hand
on rail replaced by a declaration of rust
and occasional student sitting to study
or clear the head

Strange how the world transmutes
this hedgerow crossing grown in size
its function altered from steps to stasis

background car park's destruction
acknowledging all cars are larger now
though measures of how much
we have grown less clear

is the irony that Concrete Country
no longer needs off-road 4×4s?

Postcard:
that café

Stars tonight bright as Van Gogh's.
Above the yellow café terrace
a silent firework sky. Imagine this blue/
black dome's the inside of his skull,
a brilliance of ideas flashing,
exploding, wordless throughout those
daylight canvas & oil paint hours.
All night in the theatre of his head.

P.S. All those people that I was
hope you don't think they were me

Postcard:
Arles, of course

This room contains a soap dish, towels
complimentary tissues—and this pen.
I do not know if I should laugh or cry,
nothing is clear to me.
There's a Van Gogh print next to the mirror.
For a moment felt there was someone else
in the room, did not want to admit
I know their name.
Don't wish you were here,
wish I wasn't either.

Postcard:
Aix en Provence

From my window (below the x)
the curve of the road marked with
a white line like the neck of a swan—
as elegant as that one on matchboxes,
the kind for lighting pipes.
Everywhere there are posters
of card-playing smokers, co-opted
to sell pretty much anything, though
they're rapt (wrapped?) in the game.
I can see what he meant, houses
quarried cubes in shades of ochre,
cones of cypress and a spire puncturing
this rolling grey sphere of a morning sky.

P.S. saw his last palette yesterday—
all colours exhausted except
one last squeeze of white
shaped like Mont St. Victoire

P.P.S. Came here to forget.
All I do is remember

Crimes of Passion

'A painting requires as much fraudulence, trickery and deception as the perpetration of a crime.'

Edgar Degas

It looks like they've been here before us
executing drive-by paintings, there are
Paul Nash trees opposite John Lewis
brother John has left an oak tree
on a slope in the Chilterns

on the edge of the hills
as the motorway cuts through
someone's filled the panorama
with a bravura Dutch landskip
all aeriel perspective and louring sky

in Spring Stanley Spencer's busy
every blossoming hawthorn his
Samuel Palmer's doing the apple trees
Winter, and Rowland Hilder gets to work
drawing tree skeletons on cloudy skies

in France Interpol has evidence
Cézanne's repainting Provence
Monet's working on haystacks
That copse of poplar the work of
Corot, occasionally Uccello
moonlighting from painting battles

Bridget Riley Arrives at the Doors of Perception

It's just colour you'd think
and some kind of grid, a system,
mathematics at the speed of light,
Seurat's Pointillism deconstructed
at the edge of your eyes' ability—
not so hard to decode

you understand her strategies,
planning process, colour theory,
this is discord, that harmony

complementary colours tested
vibrating, shaking our sense of balance
to near destruction

taking Degas' advice her work planned
as carefully as a crime she's plotted
for decades, this overthrow of stability

certainty, the tyranny
of horizontals, verticals
and the limits of sight

the gallery of us in this particular courtroom
waving banners of support—
a coat the colour of burnt toffee

accompanies a pink/pale blue striped tie
woman with an acid green hat
man with a scarlet scarf

those in the starkness of black and white
are her accomplices, shaking us free
from the day's becalming greyness

those certainties of which we were convinced.
Aldous Huxley you imagine
grinning at the door.

One of Those Nights

after Untitled, *Hannah Starkey,* & Cabaret Night, *Bert Hardy*

The ashtray is spotless
though smoke curls as if
from the barrel of a gun

Hard to tell which chandeliers
are real, which only reflections—
what floats, what hesitates?

In the satin darkness, unaccustomed
to wearing her heart on her sleeve
she's turned her tattooed shoulder to us

this surrogate face maybe to attract
though no danger of eye to eye
or dancing cheek to cheek

at other tables chatter drizzles
a band autographs the night

Shadows and Light

for Hestia, Greek goddess of the hearth

after Our Shadows Alone Touching You Trying to Find Where Here Is, *John Newling*, White Koan, *Liliane Lijn*, The Architect, *Paul Mount, University of Warwick campus, August 2019*

Questions regarding shadow, self and place
hanging in this ancient woodland, fertile as leaf mould
only glimpsed in passing, a metaphor maybe
for life which will plot an alphabet's course

Its your choice where 'here' is
not, of course, where your feet are
but if an archaeologist excavated you
where would your hearth be, the centre of you stand?

Hestia's cone of white ash a symbol—
home made daily with the remaking of fire,
shape of each day sat square on level ground
washed with water, cleansed with air

Not always easy to see the simple structures—
cone, cube, sphere—beneath it all,
what's essential, what is not
what can be learned, what forgotten

You might suspect some kind of architect
though he's just a man, his proportions measured out
in angles, planes, ratios, chromed against the sky
he's shiny and solid

but he dissolves in reflected clouds

Puddling

after the sculpture Reclining Stone, *Guy Stevens, University of Warwick campus*

It's not the stone that reclines of course
or geese that settle here in any weather
or water fowl dreaming foxes
but you taking up the invitation

relaxing your spine, dozing off for a while
meditating maybe
imagining yourself briefly elsewhere
favourite city, a postcard beach perhaps

moorhens and coots know nothing of this
one forever proud to be strutting
on bright green legs, the other
watching its brood of punk-feathered chicks

greylags concerned about darkening clouds
secure in the safety of a flock
envious of a coat that woman is wearing
prepared to fight her for it

monks that farmed here no longer recognise
the lie of this land, crop that's growing here now
long-gone brickmakers curious about
what clay they laboured for has built

Turner on Calais Sands

after Calais Sands, *JMW Turner*

He watches the sky turn
to flames of cloud,
burning the evening away

sea's sleeve of water
reflecting this flaring,
rinsing fanfares along the coast
to echoes of Mary Tudor's heartbeat

her ache at losing Calais
that last atom of English France
engraved on her embittered heart

bitterness stains migrant feet,
these dunes their odyssey's almost-there,
waiting for that golden opportunity,
prospect of sunrise still lighting their eyes

Hitch-Hiking

after The Drift Posts, *JD Fergusson*

can only be done in colour, starting with that
rainbow side-of-the-road smell of petrol,
dark acids of exhaust and some bright hope

for that day's destination. Roads become
ribbons of steel greys, lexicon of tone changing
with each border crossed

surface and engine noise colouring your ears,
roadside food tasting of primaries—
egg, bacon, tomato, tea strong as bracken

afternoon drones with brushstrokes of conversation
local brick and slab give way to granite and fir
road twists and turns like a painter's brush

muted blues, violets and greens roll
towards diminishing hills, surprising swatches
of sage, slate, straw and heather

with luck evening will break at the mouth of a pass
valley pouring to a sea of reflected sky
sharp and sweet as oranges, roses, memory

Postcard:
New Mexico with Georgia O'Keeffe

It's hard not to see these landscapes
as sleeping figures
taut slopes as sun-tanned curves
of shoulder and buttock
clefts and gullies the kissing of thighs
bushes sheltering those places
hidden from view
these wind-sculpted forms
breasting that oh-so-blue sky
making flesh glow

P.S. Out of the window a heron
rose clean into the evening sky

Postcard:
Colliore with Derain, July

Never been here before
but this is where I think I've woken.
The shower is dripping. Makes me
remember how hot yesterday was,
that Fauvism is true.
Some people already dressed
and in the street, daily bread under arms
or in baskets. Soon there will be coffee
and rituals like woodgrain.
Remember the aeroplane landing,
windows rattling like applause—
that's what woke me.

Regret Not Original Sin

after the sculpture This Is Days of Judgement, *Laura Ford, University of Warwick's campus, in turn referencing* The Expulsion from the Garden of Eden, *Masaccio*

Eve and Adam at the Mead Gallery building site

Roll a ball of wool and a cat will paw it
with serious instinct, claws unravel
any loose strand, any weakness

like Adam and Eve leaving Eden
that business of curiosity unspooling them
before they're sentenced

one bite, just the one and now
heads bowed and bodies dejected
the sky is falling

maybe they didn't hear Him
reconsider, that He'd been rash—
all that work—every creeping creature

this perfect garden
why despoil it so soon?
Regret not an original sin

Not daring to look back
eyes on the ground
unseen as they leave

a sign which reads
'Please Report To The Gateman'
some joker in the background

strumming a guitar
wondering in words
what's been delivered

what dreams drive us to tend gardens
plant rosemary, roses, rue
raise apple trees and apricots

hedge in or fence off
our sanctuaries, those patches
of peaceable kingdoms

take dogs and cats as companions
take life's strands and skeins
knit them into some semblance of order

For A Moment Thought You Were A Painting

Knew you weren't Mona Lisa—
your smile not so enigmatic
you hadn't lunched naked
with Manet and friends

      or so you say

Knew you'd never let Pablo
turn your head, explore
the facets of your face
Warhol make you over

      and over and over

Knew you didn't dance
for Degas or Lautrec
have Pre-Raphaelite lips
resented being anyone's

      goddess, madonna, wife

Saw your Gwen John composure
piercing Frida Kahlo stare
Mary Cassatt gentle gaze
you in the blaze of an O'Keeffe flower

Days

Georgia O'Keeffe said she painted feelings
she had no words for

bleached skulls and sunlight's harshness
shadows and hard reality

flowers as deep as swimming pools
as soft as breath

the rich and the arid
succulent and parched

like days of feasting, weeks of fasting
seasons as wide as the horizon

day after day cropped in close-up
counting mortal hours, immortal minutes

years of plenty, times of want
the wrestling of a life

Some Equations for Making A Hare

after Hare, *Regis Chaperon, University of Warwick campus*

wood + water = paper
paper + fingers = origami

imagination + materials = ideas
ideas + origami = transformation

[chisel + mallet + hands] = making

{skeletons + shells} = limestone

limestone + origami = surprise

surprise + action = hare

hare + energy = bounding

>bounding< = energy compressed

ready to spring (*S*) into action (*Z*)

thus: (H + E = *S* + *Z*) × (L = P) = (A − Ω)

where
H *is hare:* E *is energy:* L *is limestone:* P *is paper:* S *is a spring:* Z *is action:*
A − Ω *is imagination*

while
hare keeps his counsel, reserves his right to fold and unfold his form,
play tricks with shadow and light, substance and story

It's A Question of

after Black Cube, *Lotte Thuenker*

how hard is hard
how heavy the word stone
how solid a cube
how platonic

what kind of heart beats under a pinstriped suit
what hearts beat together on mattress ticking
what's carved in stone forever
what's the time frame

how soft is soft
how patient the drip of water on limestone
how long before stability is eroded
how easily our horizon tilted

what opinions are black
what are white

what's the grey area

On This Day

after the sculpture Song: Version V, *Jon Isherwood, University of Warwick campus, August 2019 (74 years and counting), for Aysar Ghassan*

Scent of mushrooms on the air
William Blake seeing heaven in these wild flowers
would know this sculpture is an opening
that there's more at stake here

Sun on our backs, us idly unpicking what it could mean
if indeed it is a symbol. Conversation rolls…
it's no secret that what we're looking at is granite, though
not hard to see some kind of bag, the way it slumps

or improbable spacecraft landed here, a mission from
some other galaxy waiting for the right moment to emerge
or plausibly a toadstool carelessly kicked, pregnant cap
about to burst, spores diffuse on the lightest of breezes

though it's not heaven in these fungi, wildflowers, trees
but atoms of a world changed forever,
particles from Hiroshima and Nagasaki planted
in everything, in all of us

And Now the Forecast for the Barber Institute

for Liz Jolly

It will be mainly sunny for most parts of the gallery
particularly in late afternoon and early evening
though shadows will lengthen over Montfoucault
a lemony light may also be visible

Further east expect it to be overcast
with a watery sun when it descends
over Varengeville and at the races
later clearing to scuds of cumulus
as the anticyclone warms

Across the Low Countries and
British Isles cloud will be thicker
with some fine alto-cumulus
and breathtaking towers of cumulo-nimbus
anticipate Turneresque sunsets

Further south skies will generally clear
and glow golden over Arcadia
with only light wisps of strato-cumulus

Across the Mediterranean clouds
may become mythical as you see
in these satellite images
there are warnings of a brief but
violent storm above Golgotha

Visitors are advised
not to raise their umbrellas
but to seek shelter in the foyer
where postcards are available